A Garden in the Rain

DELL CATHERALL

 FriesenPress

One Printers Way
Altona, MB R0G 0B0
Canada

www.friesenpress.com

ISBN
978-1-03-919855-5 (Hardcover)
978-1-03-919854-8 (Paperback)
978-1-03-919856-2 (eBook)

1. POETRY, CANADIAN

Distributed to the trade by The Ingram Book Company

Table of Contents

Winter

Spring

Summer

Fall

His Garden

Mid-summer, under a peach-ripe sky
I watch my husband from the upper deck,
slightly bent beneath a Lee Valley hat
he strips tangle weed
from raspberry canes once growing

in his childhood garden, remembers
the scratch of cherry bark on bare legs,
moonlight raids with neighbourhood boys
pocketing chestnuts for slingshots
that rarely hit their prey.

At sixty-five he hiked too far, climbed too high,
clutched his chest and couldn't tell me
he was dying. His garden,
the metronome for fibrillation.
He surrenders

to the season's pulse, the beat of the day—
capricious skies, crimson tulips surprised
by snow, bougainvillea fiesta in July,
a gnaw of squirrels, summer's lazy burn.
He hand-waters roses

for hours, spars with throaty
hummingbirds and listens to wind-song
in purple fountain grass. He's soothed
by canna lilies afire in the slant
of sunbeams at dusk.

Winter

Witch Hazel

(For our son)

Leafy batwings frame feathery petals,
sulfur beneath a thin February sun.
A rebel defies the death season
and blooms memories.
Spidery arms announce a feast
for sluggish gnats and bees who seek
redemption in the withering of winter.

Wych boughs dowse truth
in sober tracts
of frozen ground.
Brittle snow-lace tattoos,
crinkled with frost,
weave spells,
that spur grief's grip.

Manic winterbloom frenzy—
leaf buds, seed pods, flowers
crazy with delusionary dreams
heal bilious humours that haunt
bruised souls.

Forgotten, lonely amongst decay,
snapping hazel explodes.

Hellebores

You sprang from tears of a shepherd girl
who had no gift for the baby Jesus.
A winter rose in fields where nothing grew,
purer than frankincense and myrrh
laid beside the manger.

You crack through crusted snow,
shiver in shadows beneath our elm,
wear pink and mint green when days
are hoary and nights are long.

Flowers with five sepals atop
leggy stalks gaze downwards
protecting your seeds from
sleet and wind. I kneel,
admire the freckled innocence
of your disguise. Toxic hellebore
felled the city of Kirrha as
black roots poisoned the water supply.

Your toxin soothed Great Alexander's
psyche, until a traitor overdosed it
into his wine. The warrior gagged,
eyes rolling back as a lover
cradled his head. Mighty
King of Macedon,
delirious for twelve days
before death came.

Your blooms float face-up
in a shallow porcelain bowl,
an Easter centerpiece of
loveliness and deceit.

Blueberry Hill Rose

Blueberry Hill blushes
lavender
in her pewter bud vase
on a window sill
above the kitchen sink—
a natural beauty
amid seasonal glitz.
You snipped
this frozen embryo
from the garden
ten days ago,
a Christmas miracle,
a thrill, to have this rose
unfurl in December.

1957, the Grade 8 mixer,
a confusion of hormones
pubic hair and pressing
desires. I was slow dancing
with a boy
whose short-sleeved shirt
reeked of bleach
when You,
the coolest guy in the gym,
a perfect black pompadour,
tall and slim in a pink shirt
smiled only at me
as Fats Domino sang
"Blueberry Hill."

Christmas Crackers

On Christmas morning he brought gifts—
chocolates, scarves, a nutcracker
for his brother,
and laughter:
a card with a cardinal perched
on a country mailbox
stuffed with gifts,
a greeting inside
to "Daddy"
written in Chinese characters,
a mystery message
by an exchange student
he charmed at a bus stop
who giggled and played
his game.

> How will Christmas be different after Brexit?
> *No Brussels!*

He doesn't like sprouts,
is angry his mother
hasn't steamed beans.
Her idea,
riddles before dinner
in lieu of
Christmas Crackers.
He shrinks
into the Victorian chair,

a boy broken by expectations
who still wants the silly hat and toy.

Pee on the fire,
says the voice in his head.

Why is Bob Dylan's sleigh so quiet?
Family and friends shout guesses,
It rolls like a stone.
It blows in the wind.
It doesn't rock and roll.
It has 'Nobel'!
Collective groan.
What do you call a Cat in the Desert?
A dead one,
he mumbles to fake
Christmas Quackers.
She gives a hint—
Sandy, ho, ho, ho.
Sandy Claws!
Ha, ha, ha,
arms wave,
a glass topples,
red wine bloodies
the carpet, the walls,
his shoes,
a chance to bail
Get the hell out!

Unanswered texts,
love fragments
on his phone.
Did you make it home?
Turkey sandwiches tomorrow?
Are you warm?
A Christmas nightmare—
her emaciated son caged
in the witch hazel bush
he helped his father haul
to the deck
on the winter solstice,
her boy's frozen fingers
scraping an escape.
She wakes to
call again.

Once more he disappointed.
The voices know:
She'll be angry.
You messed up.
You stressed your father's heart.
You selfish boy,
a classic Christmas cracker.

Squirrels

Late January,
a frenzy of squirrels
chase tail from branch
to wire to a neighbour's
peaked roof in chittering pursuit.

You're in the recliner
reading Nesbo's *Midnight Sun*,
hiding with the protagonist
in the carcass of a reindeer.
I trim beans at the kitchen sink
while outside

arcs of acrobatic fur,
three black, one grey,
land on the Telus cable.
A game of statues
tails a silent S.
The bushy grey
flicks a swish,
shivers desire,
a black squirrel hisses,
they're gone.

In a framed photograph
beside the window,
we're twenty-three
on a Kelowna beach
leather vests, beads,
volumes of dark hair

swishing in time to
"I Can't Get No Satisfaction."
We drank cider,
bathed beneath stars
and made love under
an apple tree.
My hair now short
yours thinning and grey.
I remember days of wonder,
now missing the swish
as we teeter on
the ever-shrinking
tightrope of time.

Cold Snap

I peer from the kitchen window
past garden plots draped in blue tarps,
see rose bushes wrapped in tattered towels,
the longest cold snap in thirty years.
Aspens, skeletal under a slate sky
guard the tiny domed hothouse. A shadow
bends and stretches behind murky walls.
It's his fourth day out there,
time for the January prune, he says—
more a justification for being, think I
and worry about blood thinners and cold,
check the wireless thermometer
that sits on the sill:
outdoor -6°C, greenhouse 28°C,
must feel like he's in Belize.
I carry a glass of cool elderflower water
past blueberry bushes
their naked stems ablush in winter

and unlatch the door: a whoosh of humidity,
the smell of leaf mold and red cedar
a whir of fans. He's trimming the
bougainvillea's blooming pink bracts.
I pick a potted geranium from the bench,
admire clean cuts that shape a masterpiece,
imagine thick juicy stalks with fuzzy leaves,
crimson blossoms rich in sunlight.
Ice crystals filigree glass walls
with dandelion seed fluffs. I ask

if he remembers making a wish
before blowing them into air.
He laughs: *If they all flew away*
the girl loved you back.
Married fifty-three years, we
inhale the eroticism
of our greenhouse.
Temper winter's bite.

Snowdrops, February 2014

The day before
Philip Seymour Hoffman
deals himself the Ace of Spades
pinpricks of cold light loosen
winter's grip. Silent sentinels
spike through torpid earth,
tiny lanterns to keep
the hunger moon at bay.

A warrior actor
strove for perfection,
rescued the pathetic and repellent
from contempt. Portrayed ugliness
from the inside out,
ourselves revealed
in the creepy underbelly
of ego and self-doubt.

On a day when
white petals parted
under a frozen sun,
an unsparing anti-star
burned himself out.

Like Heuchera

I lie ruler straight, naked under a quilt
of guilt and stare into the dark, still
searching for a son somewhere
in laneway asylums littered
with syringes and trash, where
carts crash, five rock hookers beg,
and hooded phantoms kneel
in door wells digging for hope.

Nightmares from his childhood
howl in my head.
Stop!
Stop hurting me, he'd cry.
I unclenched small hands,
held my pyjama-soaked boy
tight until the shaking slowed
and we put the beast
in his head to bed.

Barren limbs claw
my bedroom window;
I walk a treacherous path,
begin to fall as he stumbles
through pain and self-loathing again.

My husband takes my hand
to stand under a snow moon
beside pots of heuchera
on the icy deck.
Broad leaves flex with frost—

pewter, obsidian, plum wine
coral bells flash silver in narrow light.
There's beauty in the saddest season,
he whispers.

A son shackled by fear,
I endure, wait for him to ring.

Daphne

Long ago I was a river nymph, free
to run barefoot and hunt wild boar until
arrogant Apollo set eyes on me
and bragged, *I'll bend this beauty to my will.*
I fled doe-like over mountain and field
chased by a suitor more powerful and swift.
He grabbed my golden hair; I did not yield
and begged Mother Earth for one final gift—
my legs took root, my arms branched out, dark bark
encrusted my breasts; long tresses became
the glossy green leaves and pink flowers that mark
the ground, where great Apollo met his shame.
My spicy perfume a fierce reminder:
Don't demean your lover once you find her.

The Watcher

Of two sisters one is always the watcher, one the dancer...
—Louise Gluck

Snapshot: my younger sister squints at me,
a tiny hand shields blue eyes from the sun.
At five, she hid in shadows under the stairs
watching them search familiar places—
her perch on the rough bark of the cherry bough
the raspberry canes behind the willow where we buried
pet turtles.
Staunton's mansion across the street.
She heard our father offer a whiskey-teared
description to the police
saw mother wring hands in guilt.
The drama played for hours
until Moira limped down the lane, one shoe in hand.
Time to be found. My sister watches,
then she acts.

I am the dancer.
A summer sugar plum fairy costumed in chintz
pirouettes on a backyard plywood stage, casts siblings in
supporting roles—
Moira, the garden spirit in mosquito netting, tosses
petals skyward,
Doug, our younger brother, brandishes a cap gun,
Let the show begin.

Three years older than the little brat.
Me, the bossy bitch.

She's stubborn—a rebel
laces her world with glass beads and LSD.
She abhors the thought of waving my cheerleading pompoms
and I
the thought of painting a brown river red.
He plays hoops and juggles ideas somewhere on the fringe
of our sisterhood.

The watcher, the dancer, the philosopher,
we empty the garment bag of Mother's vodka stash,
pay the taximan; pick up Dad with the wheelbarrow at the end
of the drive,
do well in school, are quietly perfect
and most importantly
hold onto secrets, tell teachers lies.
An architect and engineer brilliantly self-destruct
as we enable, rescue, excuse.
Maybe they'll love us back.

Privilege and neglect shape a sister,
drive her desire to affect change
with documentaries on lives lost—
women alcoholics, teens
who lose their way
pumping heroin into veins, disappear
into the black hole of forgetting.

The watcher, always there for the dancer,
a son's addiction shrouds the family in pain,
again.

Implosion.
Why him? Why us? What didn't we learn?
Guilt.
You cannot lose yourself, she says,
gives me red tap shoes.
It's time to dance.
She films my arms, my feet, my spirit,
my journey is hers,
a slow dance toward recovery.

The watcher, one with the dance—
runs through Incan streets with orphans of Cuzco,
films a kaleidoscope of twirling women in Chad,
balances her hand-held camera
as she drifts across bone-white sand in the wake
of a Japanese woman dancing memories of war and rejection.
Applaud the Queen of Sorrow and Hope.

Sisters intersect
in the heart of the city at Hastings and Main
to film the Memorial Day March honouring
missing and murdered Indigenous Women.
I bring purple hellebores from the garden,
place them in doorways where drummers pause.
Rainwater streams my face, washes my boots.
I hold the umbrella over Moira and the camera.
We follow the undulating line of quilts,
one for each of the victims.
Moira captures the moment;
I keep the lens spot-free.

Spring

Tulips

A shiver of air.
Daylight dwindles.
My gardener renders dirt with a pick
shovel and bare hands
mulching beds to nurture bulbs
until spring
when life oozes from warm soil
and stalks thrust skywards
ballooning crimson cups
atop poker stems.
Standoffish flowers
until they seductively
kick up their legs,
roll back labia, pucker
tiny clitoral appendages
with orgasmic scents
of honeyed musk.
Gardening is more than
rigid rows of perfect plants.
Only risk takers and lovers
accept the invitation of tulips
to putter in the orifices
of original sin and taste
creation's rush.

Siberian Iris

This hardy plant with spears
for leaves stands tall
in the black pot my husband
brings to the deck late May

after he clears away
messy parrot tulips,
their psyches rotted with
rococo madness.

Frantic feather fringes
drunk with colour:
burgundy stain, carmine flame
absinthe green so vivid

we kaleidoscope
with confusion until
they're spent and the
stoic iris appears.

Rainbow indigo,
three upright petals inside
a trio of unfurling sepals
etched gold with white

appliqués of tranquility,
a comfort to Van Gogh
painting away madness—
time to catch our breath.

Free Radicals

(For Alice Munro)

In ancient times
venomous flora with barbed leaves and tart, red stalks
spiked the Volga's frozen banks,
free radicals stewed in primal agar.
Greeks named this paradox "rhubarb."
Our plants, from an island brother bearing gifts,
he said: *Be careful, three sheep lay dead in the pasture.*
The narrative's in the leaves'
oxalates, poisonous when eaten,
causing nausea, convulsions, cardiovascular collapse.
Bett in "Free Radicals" used the leaves
baked into a rhubarb tart to kill
her husband's lover.

To make the rhubarb drug
that kills human leukemia cells
a researcher studying free radicals used the stalks
to prevent nausea, convulsions, cardiovascular collapse.
Parietin, a killer pigment when tested.
The narrative's in the stalks,
he said: *Be grateful, cancer cells died in three mice.*
Our plants from an island brother bearing gifts.
Greeks named this paradox "rhubarb."
Free radicals stewed in soil agar
spike the Errington farm—
venomous flora with barbed leaves and tart, red stalks
in modern times.

Periwinkle

Botanists declare
the periwinkle alien,
a threat to biodiversity,
toxic to grazers.
We embrace this outsider,
plant it in celebration
of our youngest son. Optimists
call the periwinkle *joy of the ground.*

A gardener's dream,
independent evergreen that
sprawls by the boulevard
beneath a canopy of cypress leaves,
demanding nothing.
Chaucer saw *fresh Parwynke of hew,*
five petals the colour of the sky
after a rain shower in a setting sun.

To ancient Romans it was *vincapervinca,*
bonds through bonds. A tangled
tapestry trapping poisonous snakes.
The French named it *the sorcerer's violet,*
a magic charm to exorcise evil.
I choose Italian *centocchio,*
the plant with
a hundred soulful eyes.

Our son's blue eyes,
aquifers of remembered pain,
as he paces the pavement

in every season
searching matted groundcover
for exotic periwinkle blooms,
a covenant long held
silencing furies within.

Hyacinth Blues

Apollo strummed desire,
beguiling golden-haired Prince Hyanthus.
Two lovers with grace of body
and mind scaled mountains, cast nets
in the sea then swam in the setting sun.
Both possessed a sporting spirit
sweated at quoits until a jealous Zephyrus,
God of the West Wind, blew the discus to
strike Hyanthus dead. Apollo ached. What is left
if of thy mortal goods thou are bereft?

The Sun God knelt o'er his earthly soulmate,
"Death shall not claim your radiance and youth."
He transformed Hyanthus' dripping blood
into clusters of flowers. Tears from Apollo's eyes
bruised petals purple-blue.
In *The Wasteland*, memory bore
no desire for the Hyacinth girl.
Neither living nor dead, she sought
Apollo's light and asked for more
from thy slender store,

"Give me, The King of the Blues"—
a hyacinth with a scent so intense

mortals reel as they dwell in the lap of a God.
No one escapes the blues. Newport Jazz
Festival 1956: thunder rumbles on a hot
sticky night. The Duke is almost done
when the sax riffs Diminuendo and Crescendo
in Blue. A blonde woman in a black dress excites
the lethargic crowd to a frenzy cheering: when
two loaves are left sell one

because hyacinths are forever,
each flower a spike of waxy florets
sprouting through April soil
in the shadow of our backyard fort
where fearless boys with boots played ball,
flattened flowers—a reckless toll.
In the balance of life and death
Apollo's love endures. Let the rhythm
of his blues make you whole
and with the dole buy Hyacinths to feed thy soul.

Camellias I

A camellia tree in the shady corner
by the fence, ten feet of glossy
evergreen leaves and sturdy pink
flowers. I pick a single bloom,
a gift for a Haida woman
we call Camilla. In class
she printed her real name—
Xiilaay—and laughed. *Flower
in a garden.* Graceful fingers
stroke waxy petals *like pink satin,*
she says, sticks the camellia
behind her ear.

Hair so long she sits on it—
a curtain, a nervous braid, a flirtation.
Students reach to touch, she pulls away,
silver eagle feathers on dreamcatcher
earrings tinkle. Camilla tells a tale
about a girl who came to Vancouver
with one bag of clothes, the uncle
who raped and pimped her.
She bends low, copying words:
lonely school river daughters
We write her story on lines
in a notebook until
she's squirming like a child
and escapes to smoke.

When Camilla returns
she's someone else

hacking with hands
on her chest,
a wound without a scab.
No one moves to smooth
her messy hair.

I wait for the bus at Hastings and Main;
a group spills from The Savoy,
one wearing a Stetson,
stained greatcoat, and snarl
hauls a struggling Camilla
along by the hair: *Get your ass
in gear, bitch.*
Fuck you, she says,
kicks his shin and careens
through honking cars—
a streak of black hair.
I stand and stare,
board the 16,
ride back to my garden and see
camellia flowers, pink a week ago,
edged with bronze,
ready to drop.

Camellias in the lane
like discarded tissues.
Most bloom brightly, fade fast.
Camilla hasn't come back to class.

Camellias II

1848, a bedroom in Paris,
scarlet satin and lace,
plush pillows and candlelight—
Marie Duplessis, courtesan
of the demimonde
awaits a Russian count:
your lips are red cherry bows,
your teeth the most lustrous
pearls in the world. He wraps her
in sable and kisses bare toes.

Marie, La Dame aux Camélias,
enchants from her box at the ballet,
camellias tucked in shiny black hair:
white, she's available for hire,
red, she has no desire.
A fancy Marquis ignores
her rules, bows with armfuls
of lilacs. She handkerchiefs
her nose and gasps:
Bring camellias, they have no scent.

At the opera Marie
collapses into the arms of a lover:
Armand, pardonnez moi, je suis mal.
He arrives next day in a luxury landau:
L'air de la campagne te fera du bien.
They pick berries and picnic
by a stream, kiss under the cypress
and dream someday they will marry.

Marie has never been so pure—
one man only in her boudoir
until Armand's père, stout
in a frockcoat accuses:
raped by your father at twelve,
sold to a farmer, a street slut by birth,
our family is disgraced!

Marie returns to emeralds and furs,
parties and paramours, has a bureau
with seven drawers for seven lovers.
A grieving Armand scours
Paris streets, finds his fiancée
in the arms of another.
Merde! he cries and tosses francs
at her feet: *For your services I'll now pay!*

The following May
Marie's body floats in the gutter.
La Traviata, dead at twenty-three
of consumption and a broken heart.
Armand lays white camellias
on the coffin of the prostitute
he failed to save.

Hostas

I peek through living room sheers
watch a labradoodle hunker on the sidewalk,
fixated on a squirrel splayed against
our cypress trunk. The walker aims her cell,
photographing five hostas in black metal pots.
The squirrel claws its way up the bark
as the dog yelps pulling the girl
into the periwinkle at the base of the tree.

Did she capture the diversity
of these giant cultivars?
Leaves margined in chartreuse,
cups of blue sky, twists of lime,
frosted hearts edged in gold.

Gifted from the gardens of Jane and Lynn,
our hostas root memories of best friends.
Early May travelling to nurseries
in Lynn's metallic green pick-up,
loading flats of starter plants along with sacks
of potting soil and Miracle-Gro.
Stopping by the Fraser River pub to celebrate
earthy pursuits with greasy hamburgers,
fries, and cheap white wine:
a toast to getting down and dirty.

Jane's garden, outbursts of lavenders interrupting walkways,
yellow roses smothering trellises, hollyhocks and lamb's ear
fighting for light. A generosity of exotic scents.

Lynn's garden, weeded and deadheaded daily,
pattern perfect. Magenta calla lilies, royal in raised beds beside
pots of apricot begonias, bordered by white agapanthus.

Lynn's Pantoum

Once feathery vines of white wisteria
dripped vanilla scented blooms
over life's garbage
littering our lane.

Now stripped of vanilla scented blooms,
decaying branch by moldy branch
our vine litters the lane
as rot ravages woody roots.

Lynn decays limb by moldy limb,
systems wither and waste,
ravaged nerves rotten at the root
mutate her brain.

Hope withers, Lynn wastes,
we wheel her into our garden
before her mutated brain
can no longer sense

the vitality in a garden.
Our fading friend slumps in her chair,
no longer sensing,
squandered by nature's whims.

We remember a radiant friend
freed from life's garbage
empowered by nature's whims—
a vine of feathery wisteria.

Vine Street, 2017

Our clean, wide street,
pink cherry blossoms ribbon
curbs. Boulevard giants crown
green, roots crack concrete; I know
the sidewalk well, remember when
neglected gardens flowered joy.

Rusty signs creak in April gusts,
nothing sold since last summer.
Doors hung with fabricated
Christmas wreaths, shoes
decorate porches. No one
remains to shovel snow.

What happened to hot wheels,
super soakers, the bounce
of balls in the lane? I miss
the noisy bravado of youth.
Ghost houses—collateral
for children I can't hear or see.

Rhododendrons, 2015

No place to run when Katmandu
lurches on shifting plates.
Terror rumbles down streets
glass shatters, buildings groan
screams die as temples crumble.
Rigid limbs reaching for the sky
from mountains of debris,
onlookers beg dusty rescuers
digging with bare hands
to unearth a wailing child:
buy a tee with a red rhododendron—
Save Nepal.

There's no one to save when
Charlotte sits alone in her garden
remembering hillsides of crimson
rhododendrons and the first night
they shared a narrow wooden bed
in the mountain tea house. His picture
on a table in her London flat,
No, not my son, but I love him like a son.
She was generous like a mother:
computers; village toilets; a second
story on his family home. She sent
a photo: his wife and children
wave from their new balcony.
Charlotte calls to tell us he's gone.
Her Sherpa, buried beneath
boulders and snow.

Our rhododendron isn't in flower
when there's no place left to run.
A dwarf variety purchased by an aunt
at a supermarket for a nephew
in recovery. This fragile plant
stands four feet high with stunted
leaves and stalks struggling to produce
a few mauve blooms in early June.

My Name is Delphinium

1.

Light creates colour;
we all lean towards the light.
Blue Delphiniums flutter
in sunlight, create the laughter
to brighten my dour demeanor.
Delphiniums spike upright
towards light that creates colour;
we all lean towards the light.

2.

What inspired Delphinium's name?
Greeks claimed it shared a shape
with a dolphin and named
it Delphis. Shakespeare inspired the name
Larkspur—a bird with tuneful acclaim
and a heel that resembles a spur-shape.
A withered claw can't inspire the name.
Like Greeks, I claim a sea-shape.

3.

My mother named me Dell for Andrea Del
Sarto—a great artist, but dishonest fellow.
People ask, *Is Dell short for Adele?*

I say my name is just Dell
but I share a passion with Adele
Astaire, I too am a dancer.
I wish my mother named me Del-
phinium, better than a corrupt Italian painter.

His Clone of Aspens

A clone of aspens
with knobby white trunks, you dig
a sucker sprout to
plant in your coastal garden
growing memories that last.

Trembling aspen leaves
remind the gardener of
Cariboo fishing trips
with scents of sage, lakeweed,
engine oil, and gutted trout.

His body unwinds,
loons call and ospreys soar, he
steers Misty River
along shores of golden trees:
tugging, the rod dips—a strike!

Fishing with nieces
on Loon Lake, listening
to summer adventures
fighting forest fires—tough girls
to survive male culture.

In January
he climbs our aspen, lops limbs
that rub the stucco.
It's easy to shape a tree,
challenging to raise a son.

Annas in aspens,
dueling beaks spar for syrup
from the red feeder,
feathers screech,
threatening the gardener.

Columbine Glosa

Before *Bowling for Columbine*,
a comfortable community of
familiar faces, front doors unlocked,
nothing to fear until simple
gossip darkened: troubled boys,
bullies in black coats, convicted felons,
self-proclaimed terrorists.
The neighbour's son saw a gun.
Why didn't anyone ask the question:
You want weapons?

Get up, you losers,
anyone with a white sport's cap, get up!
Shooting computers and random students
cowered under tables rat-a-tat-tat
pleas, screams rat-a-tat-tat windows shatter
rat-a-tat-tat until silence is scary
and there's no place to run
　　bang　bang　a double suicide
the massacre a bloody travesty,
we're in a library.

New Hope Columbine Library,
a space without barriers

natural light with mountain views,
students make meaning
where learning is safe
and young minds twirl
into realms beyond the imagination.
Once shaken by anguish, truth shines
authors inspire, ideas unfurl—
books are the best weapons in the world.

Twenty-two years pass. In a faraway place
we plant a canary yellow columbine
with spurred flowers rising up
like birds in flight—gentle souls
fleeing unthinkable fury:
two boys hating humanity itself.
I read *columba* means *dove,*
a global message.
War and peace live on library shelves,
arm yourself!

The Zen of Elm

(a conversation with the gardener)

Amazing, I say.
Snow falling in May . . . discs of primal
DNA blanket the ground. A big seed year
for our Lady of the Forest.

> Mythic madness.
> Embryonic pains that clog city drains,
> smother bedding plants, nest hungry insects,
> nothing but trouble from
> complaining neighbours.
> When I told Youssef it was the tree
> or me, he replied,
> *Divorce her!*

Let's embrace this elm that brushes the sky,
beckons from blocks away
and welcomes us home.

> Like you'd get lost without it?
> You know my concerns
> about roots—shallow as a wading pool.
> Envision the headline:
> *Hurricane winds claim two victims*
> *as killer elm splits at crotch,*
> *smashes through roof;*
> *former childhood sweethearts*
> *dead in bed.*

What a drama queen!
Be honest. It's more about light
reaching your precious plants.

Pardon me,
this from the woman who
writes poetry about my garden?

Our antique elm settled
long before us,
a squat for squirrels,
branches to rehab the eagle's nest
a perch for finches and chickadees,
a giant air conditioner in summer
creator of the very oxygen we breathe . . .

Relax, take that breath.
As if the city would let me
hack it down. You're right;
it's mainly about light.
I'll call an arborist to lop off
the suckers, cut out a limb or two,
allow the sunshine through.

How hard was that?
It won't be long before we're eating
barbecued salmon and sipping
a cool glass of Pino Grigio
beneath our golden canopy
spotlighted by a setting sun.
We'll be watching evening
crows wing eastward,
find balance in letting go.

Walking on Sunshine

I remember a Father's Day
thirty years past.
Our eldest son placed
a standard floribunda rose
by the picnic table
on our deck.
Walking on Sunshine,
he read off the tag
then bear-hugged
the best dad ever!

Handfuls of hope
framed by brown thorns.
This complex rose
an invitation to raise glasses,
toast barbequed ribs
and homemade rhubarb pie.
A perfect plant—hardy,
disease tolerant
with wicked scents
of black licorice.

We presented
like the perfect family
with two golden sons,
sensitive and smart, until
the younger couldn't
find roses among thorns.

Summer

Ode to the Peony

Who doesn't love a peony,
foolhardy flowers on the cusp
of summer, opening act for the big show.
Sarah Bernhardt's double cotton candy blooms
flecked with raspberry swirl vamp
in the rockery at the base of the elm.
Clean morning scents begin the day

when teenage girls with dew in their hair
giggle through your classroom door,
eager to work at benches alongside boys
with wire strippers and soldering irons.
LED lights shine names in the stars,
sirens announce: I'm here!
For what? It's never entirely clear
for girls still ragged at the edges.
Floppy show-offs for a night,
outrageous under a strawberry moon,
depressed the next day: *He broke up with me.*
Sir; I'm dying!

Every June you cut pink blooms
that bear sidewalk ants chasing
honeyed sap of teenage dreams.
Your students share the stage with
peonies placed in glass vases,
saucy *Sarah B* all pomp and circumstance
challenges the grads,
Dare to be you . . .

A Rose with No Name

Greer Catherall treasures his rose with no name—
thorny, though she be. Strollers stop to peer
at this mystery gal hangin' out in the lane.

Her bi-coloured blooms receive wide acclaim,
fuchsia and white petals make it clear
why Greer treasures his rose with no name.

Alister, a neighbouring gardener claims:
*I'll research this rose, and make doubts disappear
about the mystery gal hangin' out in the lane.*

The Rose Society reports it's a shame:
She's an orphan, no breeding—oh dear!
Still, Greer treasures his rose with no name.

Two gardeners conspire, an idea flames,
why not join *Catherall* and *Alister*
to name the mystery gal hangin' out in the lane.

The handle, *Alley Cat,* secures her fame;
the gal without a lineage cheers!
Greer proudly offers his rose with a name
to female fans hangin' out in the lane.

Mrs. Stewart's Wallflowers

She strolled the neighbourhood
wearing a floppy hat, navy,
with a tartan band,
a red umbrella in hand no matter
the weather.

Last year
she came down the lane
admired our Alley Cat rose,
spoke of the sister who gave her the brolly:
Died young, we're still very close.
You cut her a bloom,
remembered that day
she knocked
at the front door berating our boys:
Stop shortcutting across my boulevard grass!
Mrs. Stewart snipped long blades
with hair shears,
handpicked fallen leaves;
chafer beetles didn't dare dig there.
Her garden
the tidiest on the block—
deadheaded, weeded, and pruned
until
potted red geraniums
browned her front stairs.

Orange fencing, bulldozer
parked on her grass.
Amidst dust and banging,

you saved three droopy wallflowers,
planted them against our house.
Fire Kings—
glowing scarlet with scents
of honeyed clove.

Wallflowers nudge stone stiles,
vine casements of castles.
An ancient tale told
of a Scottish king imprisoning
his daughter who loved
a warrior from a rival clan.
They planned to rendezvous
below the turret at dusk.
The lass lowered by silken cord,
snagged her batwing skirt
on a bossing stone—
lost control
tumbled down
arms reaching
to a paralyzed
lover watching
her plummet
then splay
on bright
orange blooms
close to the wall.
Grief heavy,
he haunts

the highlands still,
a sprig of wallflowers
over his heart
singing praises
of his beloved.

Mrs. Stewart's wallflowers thrive
beside our gnarly lilac.
Her property a corner clear-cut—
golden dahlias, blackberry bushes,
clotheslines of sun-laden sheets,
secrets, histories . . .
loaded onto a trailer,
carted to the dump.

Bougainvillea Ballad

Greer loves his bougainvilleas,
Latin ladies from the south.
The tale of their discovery,
told here by word of mouth

Jeanne Baré was born to a world
where life was harsh and crude;
a baby wrapped in rotting cloth,
a bowl of gruel her daily food.

Although the family was dirt poor
Jeanne knew she could succeed.
Her mother was a Huguenot
and taught her *fille* to read.

Jeanne was a very curious child
who collected herbs for healing,
sold dried leaves, powders, and seeds,
word spread about her dealings.

Commerson, the famous botanist,
had Jeanne help him with his plants.
They fell in love; she bore his child,
but gave it up to sail from France.

He'd been hired as the naturalist
for a distant expedition.
Jeanne planned to go along with him,
disguised as his assistant.

Since women weren't allowed to be
aboard a navy ship,
Jeanne bound her breasts with cloth
and then in secret made the trip.

The king laid out the rules:
Find plants that no one knows,
dig them up, bring them back
for France to put on show.

Jeanne beside her botanist
explored in Uruguay,
dug six thousand specimens—
tant de variétiés!

It all went well until Brazil;
bad luck began to spread.
Commerson had open sores
and had to stay in bed.

Jeanne sweated in her shrouds
and now did all the work.
Rumours spread about her gender
which drove the crew berserk!

She calmly told the sailors:
I'm neither girl nor man.
I was a Sultan's eunuch,
working wonders with a fan.

The sailors booed and cried out,
Merde! Unable to believe,
they boldly told the captain:
This monstre has to leave.

He left Jeanne in the jungle
to disappear or die.
Instead she found a vibrant vine
that climbed toward the sky!

When she brought it to the ship,
the captain forgave all.
Flowing ropes of purple bracts
soon held him in their thrall.

I will name it Bougainvillea,
for my commander friend,
and you are fully pardoned
to sail with us again.

Colour spewed upon the deck,
a myriad of hues—
magenta, sunrise, pulsing pink,
paper-white, and blues.

The crew were quickly smitten
with the carnival display,
but when they tried to touch it—*Ouch!*
Barbed spikes drove them away.

Jeanne took a lesson with her
from the plant she so adored,
and hid a pistol in her belt
to keep her safe on board.

Then one day the ruse was up
when two men stole the gun.
They ordered Jeanne to get undressed,
said, *this charade is done!*

Commerson feigned ignorance
and cried: *How can this be?*
He is my assistant and
most certainly not a she!

This sickly man soon passed away;
Jeanne stayed in Madagascar.
Found more plants, worked in a bar,
where she met a lovely bachelor.

He, an army officer, fell in love
with Miss Jeanne B,
and when he asked for marriage,
she saw home and said, *Mais oui!*

The couple then sailed back to France
where Jeanne B drew attention;
for discovering bougainvillea
she received a handsome pension!

Jeanne Baré toiled the land
and never dreamed that she
would ever be the first woman
to sail the seven seas.

Greer loves his Bougainvilleas
dancing salsas in the sun,
and extols the bold Jeanne Baré
for all the work she's done.

I Dance

I dance to live
I live to dance,
you partner me.

I waltz with fountain grass
a blade bending, your arm
supports my back.

I tap with verbena
bacopa, lantana,
you watch me perform.

I swing with pink jasmine
vine my body to yours—
a living tattoo.

I hustle with dahlias,
fall out of step. You prune
me back.

I twirl with petunias
beneath a silver moon,
perfume your heart.

I tango with sweet peas,
improvise and return
to you.

I bhangra with golden
marigolds in my hair,
you curry my love.

Dublin Bay Rose

Uninhibited, our Dublin Bay. Red blooms on climbing canes splayed against a weathered trellis beneath the kitchen window. Stems with double-petal cups fling over the lane like high-flying trapeze artists. Prospective pickers reach up, grasp spidery thorns. Damn rose!

Our neighbour across the lane views floral chaos from her back porch. In August she phones, invites me for tea. *Come see your red rose through my old eyes*. Framed by a wizened acacia tree, splotches of green brushed with vermillion. I search the buffet and find a chipped vase, fill it with water and boughs of Dublin Bay blooms.

She forgets to brew the tea but remembers this same day in 1942. *I have something to show you*. Arthritic fingers work a black-and-white photograph from the stained manila envelope. A serious young man in uniform and a grinning girl in white satin, hand over hand posed to cut the cake. *He a forester and me a dietician living in Nanaimo. Summers we sailed the coast. Back when Haida Gwaii was the Queen Charlottes*. Faded eyes shine; she leans in, describes winds whipping up a jade sea, a crashing mast. *We almost drowned that time. Sailed up until the day he died*. She giggles as she strokes the photo, *And how he loved to go dancing . . .*

She calls the next day, tells me her husband came by with an armful of red roses.

Off with Her Head!

His Queen Elizabeth, a charming rose,
wears a sensible suit of pink blooms,
rules the garden, delights in regular shows,
will govern forever, or so she presumes.
But after thirty years he stages a coup,
complains the old girl might as well be dead—
weak roots, black spot, she's obviously through,
a single last glance, then, "Off with her head!"
Time for a new plant, fresh and untried.
Be gone faded pink; select a chic hue
place classy Black Mondo grass alongside
Chartreuse Millet with her sexy froufrou.
This fickle gardener cut down a queen.
Will his wife be next to exit the scene?

Tiger Lily

A gift of fiery lanterns with purple stipple
dangle bell-like from rangy stems
once rooted in Willy's community plot.
Generous, for a man who
sticks to himself.

Wee Willy ran from bullies
who jeered at golden curls.
Butterfly boy, they'd hoot,
used boots to grind his baby face
into schoolyard dirt.

Wee Willy wept at night
locked in a garden shed.
Toughen you up, Father said.
Shaved Willy's head, handed him
a gun, *go shoot the Vietcong.*

Willy stood strong. *No, I won't go!*
Jailed two years in an infested
cell. A victim of degradation
easy prey in a culture of power.
On a day pass, he walked away,

went north to Haida Gwaii,
found harmony and solitude
in temperate rainforests, planted
trees, kayaked the rugged coast
foraging for plants in secret coves.

Now he teeters on old legs
grey curls gathered back
with a purple cord, rheumy eyes
focus on his new friend:
Greer, I have a tiger lily for your garden.

You plant his gift in a terracotta pot
watch waxy petals curl back
on themselves to expose six tangerine
stamens with toxic pollens that stain
rust red when you brush too close.

Tropicanna in Abkhazi Gardens

We met again. We married. We lived
happily ever after. We created a garden.
    —Peggy Pemberton-Carter and Prince Nicholas Abkhazi
    (Victoria, BC)

An August encounter,
you glimpse her across
rocky outcroppings.
Beyond the Gary oak
blue agapanthus trumpets
a blood orange explosion,
instant infatuation
with Tropicanna
at Abkhazi.

Her image transfixes:
a botanical Siren,
folds of dark, taut flesh
dangerously seductive
with an exotic stalk
of spikes and flowers,
a tango skirt
ruffling desire.

You want her close,
nurture a starter plant
in a mix of potting soil
laced with bone meal.
Bed her in a tall
terracotta pot

with yellow begonias,
tuck in silvery licorice,
water generously and wait
until . . .

ruby-red spears unfurl
as variegated bronze paddles,
burgundy, pink, olive green,
stained-glass windows
backlit by the setting sun.
You let go of understanding,
embrace the wisdom
of ancient Gods. Revel
in the ecstatic.

Fig Sestina

A breath of cloud purples
the hot August eve.
He searches the garden
for a gift to excite his wife
and picks a single fig,
aged to perfection.

Hard to keep a perfect
fruit that's matured to purple.
Roosting crows peck at figs
on a summer's eve;
he yells like a fishwife
and slings nuts into the garden.

Is his fruit from The Garden?
Who's to say Adam's perfect
temptation for swiving
was red. Why not purple?
A woman as reckless as Eve
would crave a fig.

His wife doesn't give a fig
for a Mac from the garden.
On their anniversary eve
she knows an imperfect
world will bruise purple
patches in everyone's life.

Her husband, long wifed,
confidently figures
she harbours purple
imaginings in the garden.
He considers her body perfectly
delicious, though long past Eve's.

She flaunts sagging flesh on the eve
celebrating forty-five years of wifely
devotion, knowing imperfections
incite love. The fragile-skinned fig
mirrors her gardener,
as sensitive as the colour purple.

He cuts evenly through the ripe fig,
offering his wife the love he's gardened;
she bites into perfection and tastes purple.

Conversations with Anna

At a certain age, ladders become risky.
A friend fell from the top rung
digging leafy debris from eaves
and broke two legs.
Yet there you are
balanced on a ladder,
arm stretched wide
painting an arbour
as you chat with Anna.
She arrives daily at three,
perches on the power line
inspects your progress,
offers judgement
in a scratchy, metallic voice.
You look up, seek approval
from nature's flying jewel.
Anna hovers close,
flits backwards, then sideways,
lingers longer than usual.
With paint brush suspended
you lean out, eyes following
the blur of green
winging to the feeder. I gasp
as you grab a trellis, then,
momentarily bewitched by
her essence, carry on.

The Scar

My fingers trace the scar, prickly-soft,
a spiny caterpillar inching up
my husband's shin.
Last August he snipped
rusty pollen from tiger lily stamens
as Anna hummed close.
Brandishing shears of protest
the gardener stepped into air,
gravity sucked his body
into potted geraniums ten steps below.

He crawled to the top deck—
Help, I need help—
red liquid pooled his left foot,
one arm a broken wing.
I guided him to the Adirondack,
swabbed dirt from an angry gash
wrung bloody towels into a bucket
and dug shards of terracotta
from flesh. He swore
when I reached white bone.

X-rayed in the ER,
a major crack, extensive bruising,
his torso a many-coloured tattoo.
Anesthesia numbed the pain while
steady fingers worked
the curved needle sewing

a memory of the summer day
my gardener subverted
a symbiotic duet. Final diagnosis:
overcome by entitlement.

Consider a Ripe Tomato

Earthy foliage,
fragile skin lightly under pressure
trapping juice and seeds within
folds of rich, red flesh,
nature's parcels kissed by sun, washed by rain.

Heirloom tomato seeds from Portugal
smuggled across an ocean on a steamer ship,
later gifted to my husband
by the granddaughter,
a dark-haired beauty singing Fado.

2021: BC burns,
yellow blankets of foul-smelling
smoke spread to the coast,
day turns into night. My gardener
blows ash off ailing leaves.

A fine balance for the gardener—
too hot, fruits stress, too wet
roots rot. He builds an irrigation
system, wraps plants in woven skirts
to shade them.

Summer's end he presents me with
mature fruits: *Caress a tomato, inhale the sublime.*
We slice ripe romas, eat them with fresh basil
bocconcini, olive oil and toast earth's bounty
with a glass of Douro wine.

He remembers
tickling the tomatoes with the
young senhoriata from Alentejo.
I visualize
the infatuation of youth
and the art of gentle stimulation.

Chicomecoatl

I am Chicomecoatl, Aztec Goddess of Produce,
witness to genocide. Conquistadors handed
my land to the King of Spain on a bloody platter.
Swords and firearms murdered my people.
Montezuma gifted silver treasure,
until greedy Spaniards took him hostage.
Disease and false gods followed the hairy ones.

I am Chicomecoatl, trickster who reaped revenge,
threw sour golden berries into my boiling lake
turned them red and called them tomatoes.
Spanish sailors brought sacks to their homeland,
seeds spread. I rumoured the fruit a nightshade—
Beware! Scarlet orbs brought death to England,
acidic juice leaked lead from pewter dishware

I am Chicomecoatl, arbiter of culture.
My scrappy fruits, point-perfect projectiles
volleyed at actors and villains. Skins rupture,
juice and seeds spatter protesting opinions.
Rotten tomatoes can kill or make art.
I certify the freshness of Wonder Woman.
Hail Chicomecoatl, Goddess on a mission.

Red Heather

The mist rose and died away, and showed us that country lying as waste as the sea; only the moorfowl and the pewees crying upon it, and far over to the east, a herd of deer, moving like dots. Much of it was red with heather; much of the rest broken up with bogs and hags and peaty pools; some had been burnt black in a heath fire; and in another place there was quite a forest of dead firs, standing like skeletons. A wearier-looking desert man never saw; but at least it was clear of troops, which was our point.

—Robert Louis Stevenson, from *Kidnapped*, chapter XXII

I place a brown cardboard box on the lawn,
we stand back, consider the red heather
in our rockery beneath the skyscraping elm.

You recall a sunlit spring day lying on the grass in your
mother's garden reading *Kidnapped*. David Balfour and you,
two boys slogging across a Scottish moor,
trying to outrun government troops and Highlanders.
You looked up at cumulous clouds, pictured red heather,
peaty pools, a pewees cry and skeleton trees.
The next day you and the gang took bows and arrows
to the frog pond in the forbidden woods where
bully boys hid and squirrels clawed up ancient cedars—
their skins now hung from the childhood quiver
suspended above your basement bench.

At twenty-nine, driving from London
to Edinburgh, frenetically circling roundabouts
until we landed at the B&B. A lassie handed us the key:
Yoo're stayin' in Red Heaither, th' room in th' rear,

a sprig of purple-red blossoms hung on the door.
Heather flamed under the evening sun on Salisbury Crags;
we climbed towards Arthur's Seat, winds gusting
the peak, held each other close and vowed
to return and hike the West Highland Way.

I was fifty-four. There were three of us—
my friend, her daughter, and me trekking from
Milgnavie to Fort William. One hundred miles
with midges about our eyes and Scottish mud
in our boots. Rain every day until light cleaved
the blackened sky over Rannoch Moor.
I read from our Guidebook: *A spongy muir
can swallaw ye whole.* We adventured onto
a land of bog, lochans, and heather-clad heaths.
Macgregor warriors hid in mists; the headless dog
tracked our route and Caillich cursed the sun.
The cries were real. Behind a stone stele
a Hindu girl saried in turquoise and gold,
trapped in a sinkhole. *Cut. Run it again,*
the director called. The story was grim.
She and her Muslim lover, forbidden
to marry, had fled to a barren land so cold
no Hindu would follow them there.
I picked a sprig of red heather and mailed
this tale back home.

I open the box, pull out your anniversary gift,
a small stone Buddha in meditation pose. We place him
on dark soil beside the red heather and remember
the time our family lost its balance.
You stayed close to the garden,
encouraged me to hike our dream
and walked beside me every step of the way.

Fall

Soundtrack, 2016

(for Leonard Cohen)

I embrace the love
you garden,
    Hallelujah

A wet November night
the moan of wind,
our dining table
in candlelight.
A hibiscus bloom
from the greenhouse
set between bowls of
puttanesca, for the poet
who slipped into darkness
at the crack of dawn.

We dance memories
in a room with
    Marianne

The wine is red
the legs are long
the golden hibiscus flower
a song—
five petals expand,
creped wings waltz
round
a crimson core
twirling until

they drop
at dawn.

Inconstant love
at twenty-two,
  Hey, That's No Way to Say Goodbye

I went away, skipped school
partied off tailgates
in Alberta snow.
Sunny days
burned cold
without the softness
of coastal rain.
You met a girl
and wrote,
we're through.

We tried again
until I flew like a
  Bird on the Wire

1967: a Damascus hostel,
from the rooftop
a city under fire
I heard death wail,
and wired
I'm coming home.
You crossed
mountain and prairie

in a 58 MGA
to gather me
in your arms.

Truth rings strong
in the
Tower of Song

Flower of an hour
folds in,
the end comes soon.
The music plays,
we weep and laugh
bow down with he
who lights a path
through
the brokenness of life.

Pine Cone

I find a pine cone
dropped by a crow
beside the stone birdbath
where a hooded son
once hid and smoked.
Carapace scratches
my hand with scales
that shield seeds.
Earbuds blaring Iron Maiden,
he turned up the volume,
pineconed his person
against bullies
inside his skull:
LOSERBOY, be scared, really scared,
We're coming for you.
I crush the cone
and bleed.

Rescuing Isn't Advised

Get that fricking bird out of here!
My husband stands in the doorway of my study,
a brown bird with black eyes
cupped in his hands, explains
it smashed into the kitchen window,
drunk on mountain ash berries.
He asks me to google stunned birds—
check for blood, broken wings, leaky beak—
and lays it gently on the deck.
I suggest we follow Step 5 and put it in a small
covered box. Not necessary he says,
excessive handling isn't good.

I put our addicted boy in a box
with locks on doors and endless rules
to keep him safe,
doing something to fix things,
or nothing, as it turned out.
His guilt became mine.
They say Rescuing
isn't advised.

Garbage Day

Mid-October
you've been awake since before dawn
anticipating   Thursday morning's
alarm   neighbourhood invaders
peel from the pack   ravenous beasts
    rattle   roar   squeak
down lanes eating their way
to our house   belching below
the kitchen window   mechanical
arms seize garbage bins   heave
    bubble wrap   styrofoam
into the hopper
    compact   crush
detritus disgorged at the Delta Dump

In the garden
you dig raised beds   find
    stink bugs   spiders   beetles
silent machines in leaf litter
aerate spring soil
    honks   back-up beeps
announce   GFL Environmental
the green recycling hulk
    smash   clank
you retrieve the gray box
wave the guys on   one
responds   the other
scowls   you think
a bad night

late afternoon
you prune raspberry canes
and worry   our home is
missed again   the green bin's full
where will the clippings go?
    rumblings   a monster
powers down the lane
screeches to a halt   groans
    lifts the neighbour's
food scraps and garden waste
    a feral growl
the brute accelerates past our bin
    "bastard"   you yell
at the dripping behemoth
    lift the lid   inhale
two weeks of rotting fish
    3-1-1
I wish to report
a planet under siege

Toad Lily Tale

Clusters of creamy buds, covert in shade,
soon star-like petals, speckled purple. Days
shorten, nights chill. You lift the Toad Lily
up from the garden to brighten our deck as fall
dulls summer gold. How did this attractive
plant become a warty amphibian? A mystery

from the Philippines. 1970: the mysterious
Minister of Tourism reveals a shady
Stone Age tribe living in Mindanao. To attract
attention, he leaks photos of Tasadays
wearing only leaves, eating windfallen
fruit and frogs. These ancients believe lilies

help them catch food. Toad lily
juices rubbed on bodies with mystic
powers prevent men from falling
off logs into shadowy
waters where crocs lurk as doomsday
beasts. The odorous lily is a frog attractant.

Croakers jump into hunters' hands and attract
National Geographic: *Tasaday and toad lilies,
an ancient miracle.* Tourists gawk at daily
life in a rainforest. Locals plea: *Respect their mystery!*
A bestseller, a television show, doubt shadows
the story. People without fire, tools or art—a fallacy.

Scientists cite bad research; the plan falls
apart. Government fails to attract
funding as fake cavemen emerge from shadows
tired of rubbing themselves with toad lily
stickiness and mouthing tadpoles for a mystery
revealed as a hoax. *We're no longer faux-Tasadays!*

Innocence locked in time. Somewhere today
a believer will claim that rain falls
on lost civilizations. Sasquatches, aliens—mysterious
fantasies intrigue. A fraudulent attraction
caused the orchid-like toad lily,
to remain a misnomer in the shadows.

In days past, maidens kissed frogs into attractive
princes. In fall I kiss my prince of the toad lily,
grateful he gardens mystery and lightens our shadows.

Patrick Y

I deadhead brown roses in late September,
breathe the efflux of a garden preparing to die.
The chill of fall, tomatoes with blossom end rot
decay on vines; rats gnaw the remains,
spider filaments web my face,
V's of geese honk overhead.
In fading sunlight I draw my shawl,
too soon to hide inside.

A poster on a power pole yesterday—
Patrick Y, our Megaphone man is dead.
A smile for a twoonie, a joke for a chat,
he remembers days on the prairies
shooting wild turkeys and eating
his mother's bearberry jam.
I turn my Hope in Shadows calendar
to October, where did the summer go?

Begonias, October 2014

I thought we were simply removing
begonias from the ground before the killer
frost came.

Kneeling on foam
you reached deep into the front bed
dug up plants, shook dirt from roots
until two dozen tubers with healthy stalks,
soft leaves and colour-sorted blooms
lay beside you on the grass.
You sat back on your heels, chest knot-tight,
numbness snaking your arm.
We knew the signs—
unable to speak you counted beats
until the ache was gone.

On the evening news, mourners
in Saint-Jean-sur-Richelieu
laid bouquets in the shopping mall
where a terrorist rammed his car
into Warrant Officer Patrice Vincent.
Our nation grieved
while a Quebec father
wept for his soldier son.

Next day, I found you in the greenhouse
trimming hairy begonia stems,
red, yellow, white blooms draped
the edges of grey plastic tubs.
Another defender's been killed,

on Parliament Hill.
Utter madness, you said,
cradled a bulb and gently wrapped
it in the news of this horrifying month.

CBC silences Jian Ghomeshi
for secrets everyone knew—
a bully who twisted desire.
Nine women accuse
a man who never
brought them flowers.
Luke Magnotta uses
an angle grinder to butcher his victims,
encases body parts in fuchsia tissue
and arranges them in his refrigerator,
like objets d'art or spring bulbs
dripping blood.

Not a plan for immortality
you said, moisture breeds rot.
Begonia tubers must be completely
dry before they're wrapped
and stored safely in the dark.

In March you show me
furry caked-brown discs sprouting
red nodules the size of spider mites,
lift them off musty newspapers
nest them in a peat moss bed.

Winter gloom disappears,
we dare dream of summers
when girls wear scarlet
begonias tucked into their curls
cautionary signs,
handle with care.

Dianna Mah-Jones

5,6,7,8 once more from the top. Our last rehearsal before Thursday's performance. An adult dancing group tapping together over 30 years, laughing as we leave the studio to disappear into the night.

Next day the shocking news: Dianna Mah-Jones is dead. Her husband too. Broken bodies in the basement of a blue matchbox house.

Yellow tape. A double homicide. White paper suits bagging suspicions. Rumours surround a bloody hatchet, red stains on stone steps.

We saw and heard nothing, the neighbours said. *Good people. Married forty years.* Random or targeted, public vigilance advised.

A Health Care Hero where function met style, Dianna fashioned an arm, ballooned a brace, transformed broken dreams. Independently fierce, she would not go quietly under a waning September moon.

I visit our garden, snip magenta asters and drooping dahlias; cut six yellow roses; pull gnarled geranium stalks from pots. Crimson petals fall free as I lay my love on her front lawn. A bouquet of sorrow in Vancouver rain.

She'll never grow old. A blade of fountain grass. Purple hues in black hair. Strong legs, feet tapping syncopated rhythms. Forever the dancer, wearing a green silk dress and flirtatious smile on the local news.

I sense her waiting behind me, ready to tap into the spotlight . . . when I turn she's gone, her red sequined costume shredding into the wings. The music cues and I dance Dianna's memory out of the dark.

The Garden is Dying

A night of hard frost, the garden is dying.
Scarlet dahlias, crimson begonias, the burgundy
leafed Abyssinian banana—a bloody massacre,
the back yard a collection of corpses,
a scene from the Red Wedding.

> Pandemic loneliness, the seniors are crying
> caged within four walls, wheeled to wave
> through windows at fading memories,
> no one to brush their hair or hold a hand.
> *Can't Smile Without You* in their heads.

A creep of ennui, hope is dying,
re-energized COVID stalks the land
anti-maskers and anti-vaxxers march,
terrorists behead, world economies run red,
lockdown Act II: the bloody dagger looms.

> Playdates forbidden, the children are crying
> An upside-down world: stay away, keep close,
> cover your smile. The Big Bad Wolf
> locks boys and girls in a quarantine tower,
> trolls and ogres live under their beds.

My gardener protests: *The garden's not dying.*
Plants die; gardens are forever. Sleet on our faces,
we lash a rose bush still with twelve yellow blooms
to the railing and remember the recovered patient
dancing a hospital exit to "Stayin' Alive."

Bard Boy

My body's nobody's body but mine
leave it alone when you hear me say no.
—Peter Alsop

My son's name is Bryn, a Welsh word meaning little hill. The high school music director called him Bard Boy.

My son squashed a secret. Protected himself with laughter. Masked pain with cocaine.

> *You're a useless piece of shit,* whispered the demon in the
> closet. Reliving Grade 4 trauma and hidden shame
> his psyche aches.

My son wrote an award-winning essay on the importance of remembering lessons from the Holocaust.

My son sang in the church choir, injected heroin between bushes and hymns.

> A missing son's photo posted on street lamps
> in Vancouver's Downtown Eastside.
> The midnight call: I'm taking your son to Thailand
> for opportunities: I dialed the police.

My son busked *Nessun dorma! Nessun dorma!* and met his dealer in fetid lanes behind Hastings and Main.

My son's black-and-white photographs were displayed on the walls of the Justice Institute of BC.

My son pawned my jewelry, his cameras, his trumpet, his soul.
Desperate and dope-sick he called home.

My son wrote to the psychiatrist: *Lucifer says I have no respect,
he knows of all things not right.*

> Confirmed bipolar, schizoaffective, PTSD.
> *Pill after pill after pill—fuck it!*

My son had many saviours, the ballerina my favourite.

> Treatment and relapse
> the seasons of his years
> as our elder son kept searching
> for the brother who disappeared.

My son weaned himself off opiates with methadone. Ten years
of supervised visits to a pharmacy that cared.

My son found purpose and love working beside his father in
our garden.

> He secreted banded stones
> in the Buddha's praying palms
> on the rim of the stone birdbath
> in the crotch of the elm
> atop the raspberry canes—
> treasures we discover still.

My son and his brother texted daily,

Hey Jeremy, my fellow crazies are everywhere. You
cannot hide.
Soon we'll control the credit unions and then the fro yo

frozen yogurt !?!?
Yes, the hipsters love it. We've been adding chemicals to the fro yo
for years. The hipsters will be our complacent army

You should consider standup!

My son held tight to his name. Gave it to the least, the lost and the vulnerable, the deacon said.

My son reached for a crutch to climb his hill during the loneliness of Covid.

We found Bryn's distended body, prostrate in his hall.
The coroner's report: recreational drug overdose by
mixed toxicity
Cocaine. Fentanyl. Carfentanil.
Poisons in a body that was never his own.

That rainy day in November, his writing prompt:
If you could indulge in anything without
consequence what would it be?

My son had already made a silly Christmas hat for the brother he adored.

Index of a Life Lived Close to the Earth

In the beginning was Agapanthus,
    the African love flower;
spoken softly, it's almost like praying.

Bleeding hearts dangle a secret,
    the sadness of a lost boy
stumbling his way home.

Magnets for winter-weary bees,
    Crocuses in purples and
yellow crouch close to the ground.

The drama of Dahlias in raised beds,
    flamboyant actors demand
centre stage for a five-month run.

Grateful for English bluebells that
    line the lane. I hear boys
on bikes with training wheels.

Yellow branches of Forsythia
    graze the windowpane above
the sink; I wave to sons outside.

Geraniums colouring the deck,
    strains of a Puccini aria
recall a family trip to Italy.

Our knotted Hibiscus tree, gifted
    by a friend celebrating
the birth of our firstborn son.

A wreath of Ilex from the winter
    garden, prickly greens with
berry reds shimmer in candlelight.

Chartreuse elegance of Japanese
    forest grass borders the
walkway--welcome to our home.

Was that a time-step, shuffle ball
    change or simply toe heel?
He plants Kale for my dementia.

The Lupine Lady followed us from
    Nova Scotia, tossing seeds
to the wind for a beautiful world.

Boldly coloured, Marigolds signal
    celebration. In India
I wore golden garlands for Diwali.

Nicotiana—a paradoxical genus,
    clusters of fragrant flowers
or the stale odour of tobacco smoke.

Have you met Barbara Tingley?
    An Ornamental oregano,
with bracts wearing butterflies and bees.

Plantings of Phlox, vibrant performers
    against pyramid cedars
bewitching us with mystical scents.

Queen Anne's Lace, Pender wildflowers
    transplanted to Vine Street,
calling us back to the island bluff.

Rainbow Ranunculus, a blooming
    bouquet planted for Easter
in the cement pot by the stairs.

Purple Salvia and a Grecian urn from
    Alexia's garden—a sage
metaphor for everlasting friendship.

Maroon and ivory Trillium
    flower before robins nest.
I admire their resilience in icy rain.

My gardener's experiment, Umbrella
    grass potted with red coleus.
Did you pull this out of a ditch, I ask?

Verbena garden stars, our favourite
    royal plum wine with
intoxicating hints of sunlight and song.

Fluttering curtains of white Wisteria
    veil a weathered fence;
their purity inspires us to dream.

Xerochrysum, strawflowers—an artist's
    palette of petal-like bracts
with shades of immorality and joy.

Our classic Yellow Mellow Hybrid Tea
    glows in the rose bed beside
Voodoo, Full Sail, and Queen Elizabeth.

A robust orange Zinnia, last flower on
    the deck. Latin for *beautiful man*.
Like the creator of our garden.